Breakfast

IS SERVED

An Hachette UK Company
www.hachette.co.uk

First published in Italian in 2017 by Nomos Edizioni, as *The Breakfast Journey*

First published in Great Britain in 2018 by Mitchell Beazley,
a division of Octopus Publishing Group Ltd
Carmelite House, 50 Victoria Embankment, London EC4Y 0DZ
www.octopusbooks.co.uk
www.octopusbooksusa.com

Distributed in the US by Hachette Book Group
1290 Avenue of the Americas, 4th and 5th Floors, New York, NY 10104

Distributed in Canada by Canadian Manda Group
664 Annette St., Toronto, Ontario, Canada M6S 2C8

ISBN 978 1 78472 337 8
A CIP catalogue record for this book is available from the British Library.
Printed and bound in Slovenia
10 9 8 7 6 5 4 3 2 1

Photography: Laura Ascari
Illustrations and design: Elisa Paganelli
Recipes and food styling: Lorenza Barletta and Ludovica Frigieri
Commissioning Editor: Joe Cottington
Senior Designer: Jaz Bahra
Junior Editor: Ella Parsons
Translator: Simon Jones
Copyeditor: Jo Richardson
Senior Production Controller: Allison Gonsalves

Standard level spoon measurement are used in all recipes.
1 tablespoon = one 15ml spoon
1 teaspoon = one 5ml spoon

Eggs should be UK medium (US large) unless otherwise stated. This book contains dishes made with raw or lightly cooked eggs. It is prudent for more vulnerable people such as pregnant and nursing mothers, invalids, the elderly, babies and young children to avoid uncooked or lightly cooked dishes made with eggs. Once prepared these dishes should be kept refrigerated and used promptly.

Ovens should be preheated to the specific temperature – if using a fan-assisted oven, follow manufacturer's instructions for adjusting the time and the temperature.

Pepper should be freshly ground black pepper unless otherwise stated.

Milk should be full fat unless otherwise stated.

Breakfast

IS SERVED

BREAKFAST & BRUNCH RECIPES
FROM ALL OVER THE WORLD

LAURA ASCARI & ELISA PAGANELLI

MITCHELL
BEAZLEY

"Books can be possessive, can't they? You're walking around in a bookstore and a certain one will jump out at you, like it had moved there on its own, just to get your attention. Sometimes what's inside will change your life, but sometimes you don't even have to read it. Sometimes it's a comfort just to have a book around."

Sarah A. Allen

Introduction

Even before our paths crossed, we both loved the early hours, the first kisses of light on little household objects, the haze of fine airborne dust caught in a ray of sunshine between the curtains. As in a film, our daily rituals were just visible through our two windows; two magically parallel lives.

The warmth of the covers giving way to the sharp air of morning; the first cup of tea clasped in both hands. Peeping out at the day through eyes still blurred with sleep. If we had been able to describe the joy of small things, it would have been this moment, suspended in the light of a day that was still to be lived. And it was precisely breakfast that brought us together, that enabled us to discover our enormous artistic and culinary affinity. We began to photograph and draw, driven by the desire to blend our respective creative worlds and curious to see what would happen. So it was that a dream took shape. A dream that we literally put into the oven and took around the world, to discover what breakfast is like in your home – and in everyone else's.

For this journey we couldn't but avail ourselves of the services of two exceptional guides. Lorenza, a passionate pastry cook who can turn raindrops into chocolate, and Ludovica, an itinerant cook who loves beautiful destinations where the prime ingredient is a splash of sunlight. A journey from one kitchen to the next, suitcase in hand, to discover the delicacies we hadn't yet sampled, the flavours that live for one season only, the zest that a good recipe first thing in the morning can give you. There are those cookbooks that aim to teach you how to cook according to the seasons, others that demonstrate the best techniques to produce the most elaborate dishes. This book is a one-way ticket that allows you to wake up in another city, another country, without needing to change time zones!

Have you packed your bag?

Contents

Qaimaq chai

AFGHANISTAN

You are walking with your eyes closed through a magical green tea garden. The perfume envelops you as Afghani rose petals flutter down on to your head. Let yourself be comforted by the warmth of the cup in your hands.

For the qaimaq:
480ml (16fl oz) milk
90ml (6 tablespoons)
  double (heavy) cream
½ tablespoon cornflour
  (cornstarch)

For the chai:
480ml (16fl oz) water
4 teaspoons loose leaf
  green tea
¼ teaspoon bicarbonate of soda
  (baking soda)
480ml (16fl oz) milk
4 teaspoons white sugar
2 cardamom pods, crushed

Serves 4
Cooking time: 3 hours

The qaimaq
Pour the milk into a saucepan and bring to the boil. Reduce the heat, add the cream and stir. Sift the cornflour (cornstarch) into the saucepan, mix well and cook over a low heat for approximately 30 minutes. A thick cream will form on the surface of the milk, and as it does so, skim it off into a separate pan, ideally a wide, shallow one. Only a little of the milk should be left in the first pan. Cook the skimmed-off cream over a low heat for a couple of hours to finish the qaimaq. The cream will keep for a few days if stored in the refrigerator.

The chai
Pour the measured water into a small saucepan and bring to the boil. Add the green tea and bicarbonate of soda (baking soda) and leave to boil for about 5 minutes. Turn off the heat and let the tea settle for 1–2 minutes, then strain it. Next, "aerate" the mixture by pouring it from a height from one container into another several times. At this point the tea will have taken on a red colour. Return it to the pan over the heat and stir in the milk. After 1 minute, turn off the heat and add the sugar and cardamom to taste along with a tablespoonful of qaimaq. Serve with chapatis. Enjoy your breakfast!

Baked porridge

ALASKA

Rolled oats take on rich, fruity flavours and a crunchy texture. Spend a few moments with your nose in a book and sipping a hot chocolate to kick off a special day.

190g (6¾oz) porridge (rolled) oats
150g (5½oz) brown sugar, plus extra for sprinkling
70g (2½oz) almonds, chopped
160g (5¾oz) dried cranberries
1 teaspoon baking powder
2 teaspoons ground cinnamon
½ teaspoon salt
2 large eggs
480ml (16fl oz) milk
1 teaspoon vanilla extract
60g (2¼oz) butter, melted
2 apples

Serves 6
Preparation time: 10 minutes
Cooking time: 45–50 minutes

Put the oats, brown sugar, almonds, half the cranberries, the baking powder, cinnamon and salt into a large bowl and mix together well. Break the eggs into a separate bowl and beat them lightly with a fork, then stir in the milk and vanilla extract. Add this mixture to the oat mixture together with the melted butter. Peel, core and dice the apples, then arrange them in an even layer in the bottom of a greased baking dish. Pour the oat mixture uniformly over the apples. Scatter with the remaining cranberries, followed by a sprinkling of brown sugar.

Bake in a preheated oven, 180°C (350°F), Gas Mark 4, for 40–45 minutes until golden. Increase the oven temperature to 250°C (490°F), Gas Mark 9½ (or as high as possible), and cook for a further 2–3 minutes to brown the top. Serve with a hot chocolate or a nice glass of warm milk.

cinnamon

Ravani

ALBANIA

A golden cake is cut up into diamonds. Imagine seeing them fluttering in the sky like so many sparkling kites. Now, time for the first bite.

200g (7oz) plain
   (all-purpose) flour
120g (4¼oz) semolina flour
15g (½oz) baking powder
4 eggs
125g (4½oz) natural yogurt
150ml (5floz) vegetable oil
120g (4¼oz) white sugar
a few drops of vanilla extract
sugar crystals, to decorate
   (optional)

For the syrup:
350ml (12fl oz) water
300g (10½oz) sugar
grated zest and juice of
   1 lemon

Makes 10–12 diamonds
Preparation time: 15 minutes
Cooking time: 45 minutes,
   plus 15–20 minutes for
   the syrup

The cake
Mix the flours and baking powder together in a bowl. In a separate bowl, mix the eggs, yogurt, oil, sugar and vanilla extract together with a whisk until well combined. Add to the dry mixture and mix until incorporated. Pour the batter into a 26cm (10¼ inch) round greased cake tin. Bake in a preheated oven, 180°C (350°F), Gas Mark 4, for about 45 minutes, or until golden.

The syrup
Boil the measured water with the sugar for about 15–20 minutes until the sugar has dissolved. Toward the end of this time, add the grated lemon zest (reserving some for decoration). Remove from the heat, add the lemon juice and leave to cool. Cut the cake into diamonds and drizzle with the syrup using a spoon, then decorate with the reserved lemon zest. Sprinkle with sugar crystals, if using, and serve.

decorate with grated lemon zest

Lemon Syrup

Alfajores

ARGENTINA

~~~~~~

Eyes still closed, from the kitchen comes the scent of vanilla. My thoughts immediately turn to those cookies, so delicate, that.... Am I dreaming or awake?

~~~~~~

130g (4¾oz) 00 flour
130g (4¾oz) potato flour
1 teaspoon baking powder, sifted
100g (3½oz) butter, softened
75g (2¾oz) white sugar
2 eggs

For the dulce de leche:
330ml (11fl oz) milk
100g (3½oz) sugar
pinch of bicarbonate of soda
   (baking soda)
a few drops of vanilla extract

Makes 15–20 cookies
Preparation time: 30 minutes,
   plus 1 hour resting
Cooking time: 10 minutes

The dulce de leche

Pour the milk into a small saucepan, add the sugar, bicarbonate of soda (baking soda) and vanilla extract and stir with a wooden spoon over a low heat. Bring to the boil and cook, stirring, for a further hour or so until the mixture has reached a consistency similar to that of caramel sauce (bearing in mind that when it cools it will become thicker). Pour into a bowl and leave to cool.

The cookies

Mix the flours and baking powder together in a ceramic bowl. In a separate bowl, beat the butter and sugar together until creamy. Add the eggs and beat in thoroughly, then gradually stir in the flour mixture until you have a soft dough. Shape into a ball, seal in clingfilm (plastic wrap) and leave to rest in the refrigerator for at least an hour. Roll the dough out to a thickness of 5mm (¼ inch) between 2 sheets of nonstick baking paper so that it doesn't stick to the work surface (the dough will be easier to roll out if it is very cold). Remove the top sheet and use a 4cm (1½ inch) round cookie cutter to cut the dough into discs. Lay the discs on a greased cookie sheet and bake in a preheated oven, 180°C (350°F), Gas Mark 4, for about 10 minutes until just firm but still pale in colour.

Leave the cookies to cool completely before sandwiching them together in pairs with the dulce de leche.

Anzac biscuits

AUSTRALIA

A crunchy bite that evokes the memory of the soldiers who, in days gone by, were sent these cookies as a gift when they were away. These are special little morsels to light up the darkest of days.

150g (5½oz) 00 flour
100g (3½oz) brown sugar
70g (2½oz) porridge
　(rolled) oats
50g (1¾oz) desiccated coconut
120g (4¼oz) butter
2 tablespoons honey or golden
　syrup (corn syrup)
1 teaspoon bicarbonate of soda
　(baking soda)
1 tablespoon boiling water

Makes 15–20 cookies
Preparation time: 15 minutes
Cooking time: 15–20 minutes

Mix the flour, sugar, oats and coconut together in a bowl. Melt the butter in a saucepan with the honey or syrup. Meanwhile, dissolve the bicarbonate of soda (baking soda) in the boiling water, then add to the pan, whereupon the mixture will start to froth. Pour this mixture over the dry ingredients.

Mix thoroughly using a wooden spoon or your hands until you have a dough. Roll the dough into small balls, then flatten each ball into a disc 3–5cm (1¼–2 inches) in diameter. Arrange the dough discs on a baking tray (cookie sheet) lined with nonstick baking paper and bake in a preheated oven, 160°C (325°F), Gas Mark 3, for about 15–20 minutes until they take on their classic amber colour. They smell delicious! So good!

Strudel

AUSTRIA

A symphony of aromas is released with every bite of this natural sweet treat, to be enjoyed out on the terrace with a view of the Tyrolean Alps.

For the pastry:

150g (5½oz) 00 flour

100ml (3½fl oz) warm water

1 tablespoon sunflower oil

pinch of salt

For the filling:

800g (1lb 12oz) sour green apples (such as Granny Smith)

a little lemon juice

50g (1¾oz) dried breadcrumbs

70g (2½oz) white sugar

50g (1¾oz) raisins

30g (1oz) pine nuts

grated zest of 1 lemon

1 teaspoon ground cinnamon

25g (1oz) butter, melted

milk, for brushing

icing (confectioners') sugar

Serves 6–8

Preparation time: 1 hour,
   plus 30 minutes resting

Cooking time: 45 minutes

The pastry

Mix all the ingredients together thoroughly by hand in a bowl or in a food processor until you have a smooth dough. Shape it into a ball, oil it slightly and leave it to rest in a bowl covered in clingfilm (plastic wrap) at room temperature for 30 minutes. Meanwhile, prepare the apples for the filling. Peel and core them, then cut them into 3cm (1¼ inch) cubes and drizzle with the lemon juice to prevent discoloration.

Roll the dough out on a board dusted with flour into a rectangle that is as long and thin as possible. Then place the sheet of dough over the backs of your hands and use them as well to stretch it gently. Lay the dough on a clean tea towel (dishcloth).

The filling

Start by spreading the breadcrumbs over the dough, followed by the apple, sugar, raisins, pine nuts, lemon zest, cinnamon and melted butter. Using the cloth to help you, roll up the strudel. Seal the ends tightly and brush with milk. Carefully transfer the strudel to a greased baking tray (cookie sheet) and bake in a preheated oven, 180°C (350°F), Gas Mark 4, for about 45 minutes until golden. Before serving, dust with icing (confectioners') sugar. Serve with a vanilla sauce or ice cream.

guten morgen

Gaufres

It's the season of country fairs and open-air festivals, and there are scents of caramel, chocolate and crystallized (candied) fruit all around, with fairground music in the background. So this morning, breakfast is taken on the Ferris wheel!

250g (9oz) 00 flour

4g (⅛oz) fast-action dried yeast (instant yeast)

120ml (4fl oz) milk

1 egg, beaten

125g (4½oz) butter, softened

30g (1oz) honey

125g (4½oz) white sugar

a few drops of vanilla extract

Serves 6

Preparation time: 20 minutes, plus overnight resting

Cooking time: 10–15 minutes

Put the flour in a bowl and mix in the yeast thoroughly. Then add the milk, egg, butter and honey and mix together until you have an even consistency. Cover the bowl with clingfilm (plastic wrap) and leave to rest at room temperature overnight.

Mix the sugar and vanilla extract into the risen dough with your hands and then leave to rest for a further 15 minutes. Shape the dough into 6 small balls. Heat a waffle iron and grease with a little butter, add the dough balls to the hot iron, close and cook at a medium heat until the gaufres develop an inviting golden crust on the outside (about 10 minutes). Serve the gaufres with your preferred topping, whether savoury or sweet.

Bolo de fubá

BRAZIL

Saudade ("love that remains") is assured after a happy morning spent with the whole family. Today we head for the beaches of Bahia.

3 eggs, separated
100g (3½oz) margarine, softened
100g (3½oz) white sugar
250g (9oz) fine yellow polenta (cornmeal)
200g (7oz) 00 flour
2 teaspoons baking powder
300ml (10fl oz) milk

To serve:
plain dark (bittersweet) chocolate, melted
fresh berries, such as blackberries or redcurrants
vanilla sugar (optional)

Serves 8–10
Preparation time: 20 minutes
Cooking time: 20 minutes

Beat the egg whites in a large bowl until they form firm peaks, then set aside. In a separate bowl, beat the yolks with the margarine and sugar until pale and creamy. Mix in both types of flour and the baking powder, alternating with dashes of the milk, stirring constantly. Finally, fold in the egg whites, being careful not to knock the air out of the batter.

Grease a ring cake tin (bundt® pan) and dust it with flour, gently pour the cake batter into it and bake in a preheated oven, 200°C (400°F), Gas Mark 6, for 20 minutes.

Let the *bolo* cool until warm, then serve drizzled with melted chocolate along with mixed summer berries or simply dusted with vanilla-flavoured sugar.

blackberries, redcurrants and raspberries

2 teaspoons baking powder

Yummy!

Kiselo mlyako

BULGARIA

This is so fresh and tasty, it's almost thirst quenching. You feel like enjoying it while walking around the house, with the floorboards creaking and the scent of laundry on the line. There is no better breakfast when summer dawns.

500ml (18fl oz) low-fat natural
  yogurt
whole blanched almonds
shelled walnuts
acacia honey

Serves 4
Preparation time: 10 minutes,
  plus 4–8 hours draining
Cooking time: 15 minutes

Line a fine-mesh wire sieve with a double layer of sterilized muslin (cheesecloth) and set it over a large, fairly deep bowl. Pour the yogurt into the lined sieve, gather the edges of the cloth together around the yogurt to make a bag, then leave to drain for 4–8 hours.

The longer you let it drain, the thicker the yogurt will be. Once the yogurt has finished draining, the bowl will contain the sour whey, while what remains in the cloth will be a Greek-style yogurt. You can now enjoy the yogurt with your favourite topping. We have chosen a mixture of nuts and acacia honey.

To toast the almonds, line a baking tin with nonstick baking paper and spread the almonds evenly over it. Toast in a preheated oven, 180°C (350°F), Gas Mark 4, for about 15 minutes, stirring frequently. When the almonds are done, remove them from the oven and leave to cool. Chop the toasted almonds and walnuts, and mix with the honey. Now you can enjoy munching them with your homemade yogurt.

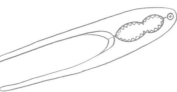

walnuts

Pumpkin tarts

CANADA

Sweet, comforting and as enveloping as a hug, these make a slow, languorous, lazy start to the day. It's a mild Sunday in autumn (fall).

150g (5½oz) white sugar

1 egg

150g (5½oz) butter, softened

grated zest of ½ lemon

300g (10½oz) 00 flour

750g (1lb 10oz) canned pumpkin, drained weight

75g (2¾oz) brown sugar

seeds from ½ vanilla pod (bean)

pinch of ground cinnamon

pinch of ground nutmeg

pinch of ground cloves

whole cloves, to decorate

Makes 8 individual tarts
Preparation time: 40 minutes,
plus 30 minutes resting
Cooking time: 30–40 minutes

The pastry

Mix the sugar and egg together in a bowl, then add the butter, a little at a time, with the lemon zest. Finally, add the flour, without mixing too much, until you have a uniform, firm dough. Seal the dough in clingfilm (plastic wrap) and leave to rest in the refrigerator for 30 minutes.

The filling

Beat the pumpkin, brown sugar, vanilla seeds and ground spices together in a large bowl until you have a smooth, velvety purée. Remove the pastry dough from the refrigerator and roll out on a work surface lightly dusted with flour until about 5mm (¼ inch) thick. Grease 8 holes of a shallow muffin tin with butter. Using a cookie cutter or rim of a glass, cut out discs of dough large enough to line the holes with a little excess. Gently press these into the holes, making sure that the edges stand a little proud. Fill with the pumpkin purée and bake in a preheated oven, 180°C (350°F), Gas Mark 4, for 30–40 minutes until lightly browned. Decorate to taste with a few cloves or, if you're a bit greedy like we are, treat yourself to a dollop of whipped cream.

cloves

lemon

pumpkin

Noodle soup

CHINA

Stop at one of those little booths where they cook nests of noodles. It's an intoxicating breakfast to eat as you wander along.

950ml (32fl oz) vegetable stock
4 large leaves of Chinese (Napa)
    cabbage, cut into strips
handful of spinach (about
    10 leaves)
100g (3½oz) wheat noodles
50g (1¾oz) tofu, diced
small bunch of chives, chopped
1 shallot, finely chopped
1 tablespoon Chinese black
    vinegar
roughly chopped coriander
    (cilantro)
pinch of crushed dried chilies, or
    finely chopped green chili
salt

Heat the stock in a saucepan large enough to accommodate all the ingredients. Add the cabbage and spinach, and bring to the boil, then leave to cook for a few minutes until the vegetables are softened. Add the noodles and cook until half done, in line with the packet instructions.

Add the tofu, chives and shallot, and season with salt. Cook for a further minute or until the noodles are cooked, and then turn off the heat. Pour the soup into 2 bowls, add the black vinegar, and season to taste with a little coriander (cilantro) and chili.

This is a vegetarian version of this tasty soup. If you prefer strong flavours, you can replace the tofu with minced (ground) pork, adding it to the stock as soon as it's hot and then continuing with the recipe as above. Choose and enjoy whichever version you like best!

Serves 2
Preparation time: 10 minutes
Cooking time: 15 minutes

a small bunch of chives

Kimchi

KOREA

*I spin the globe, close my eyes, put my finger on it and... it's Korea. Today is going to be hot!
This is an adventure spiced up with soy sauce, chili and a touch of fresh ginger.*

2 Chinese (Napa) cabbages

65g (2¼oz) salt

3 tablespoons anchovy paste

2 tablespoons soy sauce

2 tablespoons chili paste

50-100g (1¾-3½oz) chili powder

1 shallot, chopped

30g (1oz) garlic cloves, finely
    chopped

30g (1oz) fresh root ginger, peeled
    and grated

500g (1lb 2oz) carrots, peeled and
    cut into chunks

Serves 4–6

Preparation time: 3–7 days

Chop the cabbages into 3–4cm (1¼–1½ inch) pieces and place in a large ceramic bowl. Add the salt and mix with your hands. Fill the bowl with water so that the cabbage is completely covered. Cover the bowl with a plate and leave to stand overnight. Next day, drain the water. In a larger bowl, mix together the anchovy paste, soy sauce, chili paste, chili powder (the exact quantity depending on how hot you want the kimchi to be), shallot, garlic, ginger and carrots. Finally, add the cabbage and thoroughly mix with your hands. Pack the kimchi into one or more sterilized airtight jars and seal. It will soon start to ferment.

Leave to rest in a cool place for 2–6 days until it has reached the level of acidity you desire. Taste it from time to time, and enjoy it when it is how you like it.

Once opened, store the jar in the refrigerator. It will keep for up to 4 weeks.

chopped carrots

Strawberry jam

CORSICA

Fresh as the waves that break against the sides of a wooden boat and as essential as the surrounding wild landscape, strawberries star in this breakfast that takes place midway between France and Italy.

500g (1lb 2oz) ripe strawberries
200g (7oz) white sugar
1 tablespoon lemon juice
a few slices of bread

Serves 2–4
Preparation time: 10 minutes
Cooking time: 35 minutes

Wash the strawberries, hull them and cut them in half. Place them in a stainless steel saucepan along with the sugar and lemon juice.

Mix well and bring to the boil. Cover with a lid and cook over a medium heat, without stirring, for 30 minutes. Leave to cool. Meanwhile, toast the bread. You can spread the preserve directly on the bread, or butter the bread first.

ripe strawberries

made with ♥

Cuban bread rolls

CUBA

Serve these with a glass of milk flavoured with cinnamon. The warm aroma from the cinnamon combines with a savoury flavour to take us straight into the most traditional of casas particulares.

For the bread rolls:

1 tablespoon fast-action dried yeast (instant yeast)

3 tablespoons warm water

3 tablespoons white sugar

500g (1lb 2oz) strong white flour

75g (2¾oz) butter, diced

1 teaspoon salt

250ml (9fl oz) milk

1 egg, beaten

Makes 14 rolls

Preparation time: 20 minutes, plus 1 hour 10 minutes rising/resting

Cooking time: 15 minutes

Dissolve the yeast in the measured warm water in a jug (pitcher), then add the sugar. Mix the yeast mixture with the flour, butter, salt and milk until the mixture forms a dough.

Place the dough in a clean, lightly greased bowl, cover and leave to rise in a warm place for an hour. Transfer the dough to a work surface dusted with flour and divide it into 14 small balls. Place the balls on a greased baking tray (cookie sheet) and make 2 small incisions on the top of each. Brush with the beaten egg and leave to rest for a further 10 minutes.

Bake in a preheated oven, 180°C (350°F), Gas Mark 4, for about 15 minutes until golden brown. Split and fill your rolls with slices of cooked ham, and serve with a glass of milk flavoured with cinnamon, to taste, for a classic Cuban breakfast.

1 egg beaten

3 tablespoons sugar

Kanelsnegle

DENMARK

A sprinkling of sugar on a dreary day when you need to feel pampered. Then a walk past brightly coloured houses in the cold of a Danish morning.

25g (1oz) fast-action dried yeast (instant yeast)
250ml (9fl oz) warm milk
2 tablespoons vegetable oil
1 tablespoon white sugar
1 teaspoon salt
3 tablespoons ground cinnamon
400g (14oz) 00 flour
75g (2¾oz) butter, softened
75g (2¾oz) brown sugar

Makes 10–12 slices
Preparation time: 30 minutes, plus 1½ hours rising
Cooking time: 12–15 minutes

Dissolve the yeast in the warm milk in a large bowl. Add the oil, white sugar, salt and 1 tablespoon of the cinnamon and mix well. Add the flour, a little at a time, until you have a firm, smooth dough. Place the dough in a large, lightly greased bowl, cover with a clean tea towel (dishcloth) and leave to rise in a warm place until it has doubled in size. This will take about an hour.

In a smaller bowl, beat the rest of the cinnamon into the butter with the brown sugar. When the dough is ready, roll out into a rectangle about 40 x 50cm (16 x 20 inches). Using a spatula, spread the butter and cinnamon mixture over the dough, then roll up the dough and cut it into 10–12 slices. Lay the slices on a baking tray (cookie sheet), cover with the tea towel and leave to rise for a further 30 minutes.

Bake in a preheated oven, 220°C (425°F), Gas Mark 7, for 12–15 minutes. Leave to cool, then sprinkle with sugar to serve.

flour

cinnamon

SUGAR

Bolón de verde

ECUADOR

Here, wonderful scents and aromas bring to mind forests thick with mangroves, plantain trees and pink flamingos.

2 large green plantains
1 teaspoon crushed dried chilies
200g (7oz) semi-hard cheese
(such as Provolone), diced
or grated
200g (7oz) pancetta, diced
vegetable oil, for frying
salt

Serves 2
Preparation time: 10 minutes,
plus 2 hours resting
Cooking time: 40 minutes

Remove the ends of the plantains, slice through the skin lengthways and cut them in half. Boil in salted water for about 30 minutes.

The skins will have come off almost completely. Discard the skins and blitz the flesh in a blender. If the result is too firm, add a little of the water used to cook the plantains. Add the chilies and a pinch of salt, then leave the mixture to rest in the refrigerator for 2 hours.

Shape the mixture into small balls, then push into the centre of each a little grated or small piece of cheese and a piece of pancetta, sealing the mixture around the filling. Fry the *bolón* in hot oil until golden all over, then enjoy them with a fried egg and the freshest fruit juice.

1 teaspoon of crushed dried chilies

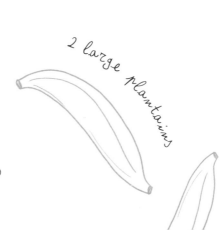

2 large plantains

Buenos!

Ful medames

EGYPT

Exploring new flavours can turn into an adventure. The sourness of lemon, the sweet spiciness of paprika. These are just a couple of the flavourings used – there are plenty more to enjoy.

500g (1lb 2oz) dried broad
   (fava) beans
2 tomatoes, chopped
1 white onion, chopped
juice of 1 lemon
1 garlic clove, crushed
small bunch of flat leaf parsley
extra virgin olive oil
chili powder
ground cumin
sweet paprika
salt

To serve:
white onion, chopped
tomato, chopped
flat leaf parsley

Serves 4–6
Preparation time: 10 minutes,
   plus overnight soaking
Cooking time: 2 hours

Soak the beans in cold water overnight. Drain them, then boil in plenty of fresh water in a saucepan, stirring frequently, for at least 2 hours, depending on the consistency you like (if you want a creamy result, blitz some of the cooked beans in a blender). Turn off the heat, then season with salt and add the tomatoes, onion, lemon juice, garlic, some chopped parsley, and finally extra virgin olive oil and the spices to taste. Mix well and pour into a serving bowl.

Garnish with a little chopped onion and tomato and a few parsley leaves. If you wish, serve with hard-boiled eggs and warm pitta bread.

Tasty!

add the crushed garlic and spices to taste

Bibingka

PHILIPPINES

Christmas in the Philippines begins with a cascade of coconut confetti and rice flour. Little cakes prepared in the blink of an eye, ready to be scoffed with a smile.

200g (7oz) rice flour
1 teaspoon baking powder
1 teaspoon salt
3 eggs
150g (5½oz) brown sugar
75g (2¾oz) butter, melted
300ml (10fl oz)
    coconut milk
desiccated coconut, for
    sprinkling

Makes 8 cakes
Preparation time: 15 minutes
Cooking time: 20–25 minutes

Mix the rice flour, baking powder and salt together in a bowl. In a larger bowl, beat the eggs with a fork, then add the sugar and mix well. Stir in the melted butter. Add the flour mixture and coconut milk alternately to the egg mixture, stirring thoroughly, with a whisk if you prefer, until the ingredients are well mixed. Line 8 holes (7cm/2¾ inches in diameter) of a muffin tin with muffin paper cases (baking cups). Pour the batter into the cases and sprinkle with a little desiccated coconut. Bake in a preheated oven, 180°C (350°F), Gas Mark 4, for 20–25 minutes until golden brown. Serve warm, brushed with a little melted butter and sprinkled with desiccated coconut or accompanied by a light coconut sauce.

decorate with a little desiccated coconut

Pain au chocolat

FRANCE

The Eiffel Tower in the distance, the smell of fresh coffee and this pain au chocolat in your hand. It's a new day in Paris.

250g (9oz) 00 flour
250g (9oz) strong white flour
20g (¾oz) fast-action dried
   yeast (instant yeast)
300g (10½oz) butter
50g (1¾oz) white sugar
125ml (4fl oz) milk
125ml (4fl oz) water
seeds from ½ vanilla pod (bean)
10g (¼oz) salt
100g (3½oz) plain dark
   (bittersweet) chocolate,
   broken into 16 lengths
1 egg, beaten

Makes 8 pastries
Preparation time: 2½ hours,
  plus 24 hours resting
Cooking time: 15 minutes

Put the flours, yeast, 50g (1¾oz) of the butter, the sugar, milk, measured water and vanilla seeds in a bowl and mix together. Knead the mixture vigorously until you have a firm dough, then add the salt and continue kneading until the dough is smooth and firm. Seal in clingfilm (plastic wrap) and leave to rest in the refrigerator for a day (it is advisable to prepare the dough the morning of the day before baking).

Flatten the remaining butter as much as possible between 2 sheets of nonstick baking paper with a rolling pin. Roll the dough out on a well-floured work surface. Place the butter in the centre and fold in the edges of the dough to cover.

Roll the dough out into a rectangle. Fold the bottom third up and the top third down, press the edges with the rolling pin to seal and make a quarter turn. Repeat, cover with clingfilm and return to the refrigerator for 30 minutes. Repeat twice more.

Roll the dough out and cut it into 4 rectangles, then into 8 squares. Place two lengths of chocolate on each square of dough, then fold the dough in on itself to enclose it completely. Transfer to a baking tray (cookie sheet), brush with beaten egg and bake in a preheated oven, 180°C (350°F), Gas Mark 4, for 15 minutes.

dark chocolate

Welsh rarebit

A golden cascade pierces the gloom of the Welsh sky on a rainy morning. It's melted Cheddar cheese with mustard and Worcestershire sauce to brighten up the day.

250g (9oz) Cheddar cheese,
    grated
90ml (6 tablespoons) milk
2 teaspoons mustard powder
2 teaspoons Worcestershire sauce
4 slices of bread
40g (1½oz) butter, softened
salt and pepper

To serve:
flat leaf parsley
red chilies

Serves 2–4
Preparation time: 5 minutes
Cooking time: 15 minutes

Melt the grated Cheddar in a small saucepan with the milk. Remove from the heat, add the mustard powder and Worcestershire sauce and mix well. Season with salt and pepper. Return to the heat and cook for a few minutes until the mixture thickens.

Meanwhile, grill (broil) the bread in a preheated oven, 200°C (400°F), Gas Mark 6, for 1-2 minutes on each side, then spread with the softened butter and cover with the cheese mixture. Return to the oven and grill (broil) for a further 2-3 minutes until you have a thin golden crust. Serve sprinkled with parsley leaves and red chilies to garnish, if you wish.

2 teaspoons mustard powder, sliced bread

Pumpernickel

GERMANY

~~~

A difficult morning lies ahead and you have a lot to do. Today you need something strong on energy and flavour. You know it already: you'll start this long day with a smile.

~~~

500g (1lb 2oz) rye flour
250g (9oz) wholemeal
    (whole-wheat) flour
45g (1½oz) wheatgerm
150g (5½oz) bulgur wheat
2 teaspoons salt
2 tablespoons treacle (molasses)
950ml (32fl oz) warm water
1 tablespoon olive oil

Serves 10
Preparation time: 15 minutes,
    plus 72 hours total resting
Cooking time: 4 hours
    40 minutes

olive oil

flour

Mix the flours, wheatgerm, bulgur and salt together in a large bowl. In a separate bowl, dissolve the treacle (molasses) in the warm water and stir in the olive oil. Add to the dry mixture and mix to produce a firm dough. Divide the dough between 2 deep, greased loaf tins.

Cover with lightly greased clingfilm (plastic wrap) and place the tins in a dry, dark place for 48 hours. When ready to bake, replace the clingfilm with foil. Place a large roasting tin three-quarters full of water in the bottom of a preheated oven, 110°C (225°F), Gas Mark ¼, and leave it there until the bread has been baked, to ensure that it's sufficiently moist.

Bake the 2 loaves for 4 hours, then increase the oven temperature to 160°C (325°F), Gas Mark 3, uncover and bake for a further 40 minutes or so until a crust forms. Remove and leave to cool completely, then transfer the loaves to a plastic bag and leave to stand for 24 hours before eating. Serve your bread cut into slices and buttered, with a fried egg, cheese and traditional frankfurters, lightly grilled (broiled).

FRIED EGG

Cook the egg in
a small skillet

SALTE PEPPER

Miso soup

JAPAN

~~~~~~

Scents of Japan fill the room. A warm, comforting soup to be savoured while you imagine you're walking among cherry blossom wearing a kimono.

~~~~~~

2 carrots

1 mooli (daikon)

2.5cm (1 inch) piece of fresh
    root ginger

1 leek

1 dried wakame leaf

800ml (27fl oz) water

50g (1¾oz) miso powder

200g (7oz) firm tofu, diced

Serves 5–6
Preparation time: 15 minutes
Cooking time: 30 minutes

Peel all the vegetables and chop finely. Let the wakame leaf soak in a little cold water for a few minutes until softened. Drain and cut it into small strips, then add to the vegetables in a saucepan. Pour over the measured water, making sure the vegetables are covered, bring to a simmer and cook for about 20 minutes.

Use a few spoonfuls of the cooking water from the vegetables to dissolve the miso in a small bowl. Add the dissolved miso to the vegetables and cook for a further 5 minutes until the vegetables are cooked. Just before serving, add the tofu. You could serve the soup with a small bowl of steamed basmati rice.

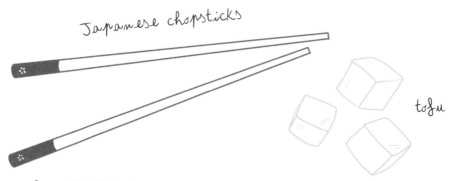

Japanese chopsticks

tofu

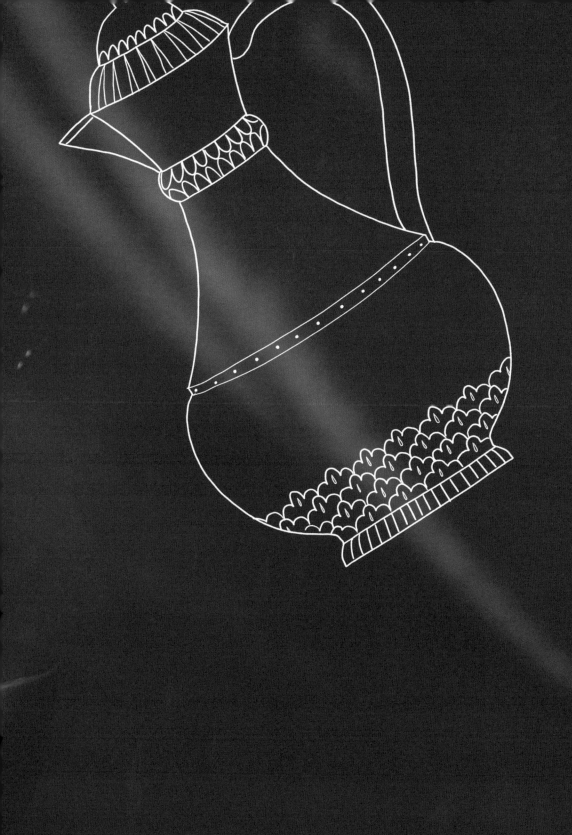

Masala chai

INDIA

It is always time for tea, and even better if that tea transports us across borders thanks to the "karha", the mixture of spices, used to flavour it.

4 cardamom seeds
4 cloves
1 teaspoon ground cinnamon
1 teaspoon ground ginger
500ml (18fl oz) water
60ml (4 tablespoons) milk
20g (¾oz) loose leaf Indian black tea, such as Assam
brown sugar, for sweetening (optional)

Serves 2
Preparation time: 10 minutes
Cooking time: 15 minutes

First, prepare the karha spice mixture. Crush the cardamom seeds and then mix them with the cloves, cinnamon and ginger. Pour the measured water and milk into a saucepan and bring to a simmer. Add the tea and spice mixture, stir well and then simmer for 10 minutes. Remove from the heat, strain and serve.

Masala chai can be served without sugar, or sweetened to taste with brown sugar.

karha

cloves

Moraba-ye havij

IRAN

The intoxicating aroma of spices gives this recipe an irresistible heady touch, like a walk through a cardamom field!

700g (1lb 9oz) carrots
6-8 cardamom pods
500ml (18fl oz) water
500g (1lb 2oz) white sugar
juice of 2 oranges and some
    of the rind, finely sliced
juice of 1 lemon
1 tablespoon rosewater

Makes 2 x 500g (1lb 2oz) jars
Preparation time: 20 minutes
Cooking time: 45 minutes

Peel the carrots and then julienne them using a peeler or food processor. Gently crush the cardamom pods so that the seeds remain inside.

Pour the measured water into a large saucepan, add the sugar, orange rind and cardamom and stir over a low heat until the sugar has dissolved. Bring to the boil, stirring frequently, and cook for about 5 minutes. Then cook for a further 5 minutes until the liquid becomes syrupy. Add the carrots and return to the boil, then reduce the heat and simmer for about 15–20 minutes until they are soft. Add the citrus juices and rosewater and boil for 2 minutes. Remove from the heat. Transfer to clean airtight jars, removing the cardamom pods.

If you prefer a spicy result, add a small stick of cinnamon while cooking, removing it with the cardamom pods.

Serve with bread and fresh cheese, such as paneer. You'll marvel at the taste when the sweetness of the jam meets the savouriness of the bread and cheese. Accompany with a refreshing cup of tea.

cardamom pods

Hafragrautur

ICELAND

Nutritious and balanced, this is a breakfast to help face the long, cold Icelandic days among geysers and puffins in the land of ice.

600ml (20fl oz) milk

300g (10½oz) porridge (rolled) oats

pinch of salt

60g (2¼oz) brown sugar

1 teaspoon ground cinnamon

1 teaspoon vanilla extract

To serve:

maple syrup

almonds

ground cinnamon

a selection of fresh fruit

Serves 4
Preparation time: 5 minutes
Cooking time: 7–8 minutes

Gently bring the milk to the boil in a saucepan, add the oats and salt and continue cooking, stirring, for a further 5 minutes.

Remove from the heat and stir in the brown sugar, cinnamon and vanilla extract. Cover with a clean tea towel (dishcloth) and leave to rest for 2 minutes.

Serve your Icelandic breakfast in a nice bowl drizzled with some maple syrup. If you like, you can also add a few almonds, a sprinkling of cinnamon and some fresh fruit.

1 teaspoon vanilla extract

brrr

IT'S COLD OUTSIDE

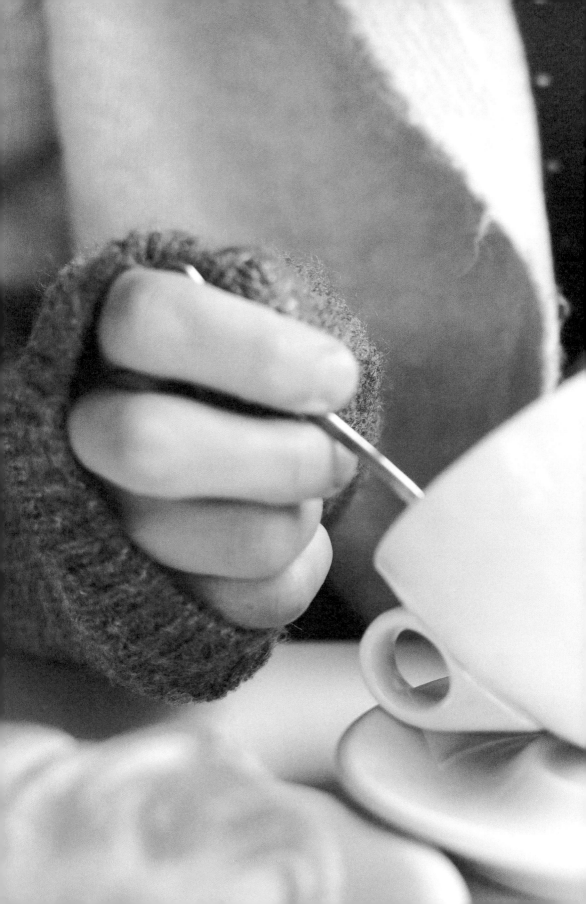

Brioches

ITALY

Shall we have breakfast at home or in the bar? One thing's for certain: breakfast will be sweet. Think of crème pâtissière secreted inside a delicious brioche. And a cappuccino, then maybe an espresso later on to really kick off the day.

150g (5½oz) 00 flour
100ml (3½fl oz) milk
20g (¾oz) fast-action dried yeast
   (instant yeast)
350g (12oz) strong white flour
1 egg, plus 1 extra, beaten, to glaze
3 egg yolks
100g (3½oz) white sugar
35g (1¼oz) honey
125g (4½oz) butter, softened
grated zest of 1 orange
seeds from 1 vanilla pod (bean)
10g (¼oz) salt

Makes 12 brioches
Preparation time: 30 minutes,
   plus 27 hours rising
Cooking time: 15 minutes

First of all you need to prepare the biga (starter). Mix the flour with the milk and yeast in a bowl, cover with clingfilm (plastic wrap) and leave to stand until doubled in volume (this will take about an hour).

Mix the biga with the strong flour, egg, yolks, sugar and honey in a large bowl. Knead into an elastic dough on a work surface dusted with flour, adding the butter a little at a time. Finally, add the orange zest, vanilla seeds and salt. Continue to knead until you have a smooth, soft dough. Place in a bowl, cover with clingfilm and leave to stand for 24 hours.

Shape the dough into brioches, each weighing about 40–50g (1½–1¾oz), and leave to rise on a baking tray (cookie sheet) for a further 2 hours, keeping them covered. Brush them with the beaten egg and bake in a preheated oven, 180°C (350°F), Gas Mark 4, for 15 minutes. Glaze your brioches with warm syrup, made from heating sugar and water (see page 18), and add a filling of choice, such as lemon curd, crème pâtissière or berries.

The grated zest of an orange

To start the day well, all you need is a cappuccino, brioche, and A SMILE!

ciao!

Rupjmaize

LATVIA

~~~~~~

Crunchy and aromatic, and dark as the Riga night, the crust of this bread conceals an unexpected softness within.

~~~~~~

470g (1lb 1oz) strong white flour
100g (3½oz) rye flour
1 teaspoon fast-action dried yeast (instant yeast)
360ml (12½fl oz) water at room temperature
2 tablespoons agave syrup
10g (¼oz) salt
2 tablespoons cumin seeds

Serves 10–12
Preparation time: 20 minutes, plus 5 hours 20 minutes rising
Cooking time: 40–45 minutes

Begin by making the starter. Mix together 120g (4¼oz) of the strong flour, the rye flour, ½ teaspoon of the yeast, the measured water and the agave syrup in a bowl to make a light paste. In a separate large bowl, mix the remaining ingredients together. Add the starter and mix together without kneading. Cover with clingfilm (plastic wrap) and leave to rise for 2 hours.

Knead the dough thoroughly on a work surface dusted with flour, then leave to rest for a further 20 minutes, covered as before. Knead for another 5 minutes, then leave to stand for another hour to rise. Repeat this last kneading and rising process again, then shape the dough into a wide loaf on a baking tray (cookie sheet) and leave to rise for a final hour. Make a couple of cuts in the top of the loaf and bake in a preheated oven, 200°C (400°F), Gas Mark 6, for 40–45 minutes. Serve with ham, salted butter and ķimeņu siers (Latvian cheese with cumin).

AGAVE
syrup

2 tablespoons of cumin seeds

Labneh

LEBANON

Sweet or savoury? This delicious cheese goes equally well with bold and spicy flavours or with sweet preserves, jams or dried fruit. This morning, discover all its nuances.

500g (1lb 2oz) whole natural
    yogurt
½ teaspoon salt

Serves 2–4
Preparation time: 12–48 hours

Line a fine-mesh wire sieve with a piece of sterilized muslin (cheesecloth) and set it over a large, fairly deep bowl. Mix the yogurt with the salt, then pour into the lined sieve and fold the edges of the cloth over the yogurt to cover. Leave to drain for at least 12 hours, depending on the consistency you like; if you prefer it thicker, leave it to drain for up to 48 hours. The yogurt will have lost its liquid and be transformed into a delicious cheese.

Serve with olive oil and herbs such as thyme or mint, or the traditional spice mixture called za'atar, along with pitta bread, tomatoes, cucumbers and olives. You can also shape the cheese into little balls and store in a sterilized airtight jar covered with olive oil, here as well adding a few spices or herbs to taste. Stored on a cool shelf, they will keep for several months.

Za'atar spices, pitta bread, tomatoes, cucumbers and olives!

Msemmen

MOROCCO

It's early morning and already it's getting hot outside. If you can't sleep, amuse yourself by preparing msemmen for the whole family. Enjoy these with a reinvigorating glass of mint tea.

250g (9oz) plain
(all-purpose) flour
250g (9oz) semolina flour, plus
extra for dusting
pinch of salt
250ml (9fl oz) warm water
120ml (4fl oz) sunflower oil, plus
extra for oiling
150g (5½oz) butter

Makes 6 msemmen
Preparation time: 15 minutes,
plus 15 minutes resting
Cooking time: 5–10 minutes

Mix the flours together and pile them up on your work surface. Add the salt and mix in, adding the measured warm water as you do so. Knead the dough well until it is smooth, even, and firm. Oil your hands lightly, then divide the dough into 6 pieces and shape each into a little ball.

Oil the balls and let them rest for 15 minutes covered with clingfilm (plastic wrap). Melt the butter and mix it with the oil in a bowl. Keep a little semolina flour nearby. Take each of the balls in turn and stretch it until you have a thin disc of dough. Brush with the oil and butter mixture, dust with semolina flour and fold the edges inward to form a square. Slightly flatten the square with your oiled hands. Oil a hot cast-iron frying pan and cook the squares in batches – for 1–2 minutes on each side until golden brown. Serve the *msemmen* hot and cut into triangles, with butter, jam and a good mint tea.

mint tea

Appeltaart

NETHERLANDS

The intoxicating scent of cinnamon is released while baking this tart, which will transport you to among the windmills and tulips in bloom.

300g (10½oz) fine plain
(all-purpose) flour
100g (3½oz) white sugar
1 egg
200g (7oz) butter, chilled
and diced
pinch of salt
seeds from 1 vanilla pod (bean)
1kg (2lb 4oz) sour green apples
(such as Granny Smith)
100g (3½oz) raisins
2 tablespoons ground cinnamon
juice of ½ lemon
50g (1¾oz) brown sugar
3 tablespoons cornflour
(cornstarch)

Serves 10–12
Preparation time: 45 minutes,
plus 45 minutes resting
Cooking time: 1 hour 20
minutes

The pastry

Mix the flour and white sugar together in a bowl. Beat the egg and add three-quarters of it to the flour mixture, reserving the remainder. Add the butter, salt and vanilla seeds and mix together to make a firm dough. Cover with clingfilm (plastic wrap) and leave to rest in the refrigerator for 45 minutes.

The filling

Meanwhile, peel and core the apples, then dice them. Put them in a large bowl with the raisins, cinnamon, lemon juice, brown sugar and half the cornflour (cornstarch). Leave to rest for about 15 minutes, stirring from time to time.

Grease a 22cm (8½-inch) round deep tart tin or use a cake tin. Roll the dough out and use about three-quarters of it to line the tin. Cover this dough with the remaining cornflour and pour the apple filling over it, holding back the juice. Cut the remaining dough into 1cm (½ inch) strips and lay them in a criss-cross pattern over the filling. Brush with the reserved beaten egg and bake in a preheated oven, 170°C (340°F), Gas Mark 3½, for 1 hour 20 minutes. Enjoy your tart warm or cold, with ice cream or whipped cream.

sour green apples

Pastéis de nata

PORTUGAL

Warm bedsheets and loving hugs. Breakfast in bed ensures that you start the day in the best possible way.

3 egg yolks
50g (1¾oz) white sugar
100ml (3½fl oz) double or single (heavy or light) cream
1 sheet of ready-rolled puff pastry
ground cinnamon and/or icing (confectioners') sugar, for dusting

Makes 8–10 tarts
Preparation time: 30 minutes
Cooking time: 20 minutes

The custard
To prepare the custard using a bain-marie, pour a little water into a small saucepan and bring to a simmer. Put the yolks and sugar in a heatproof bowl and set over the pan (or use a double boiler), then stir with a whisk. Continue to stir with the whisk while you add the cream a little at a time. Check the temperature of the custard with a thermometer, and when it reaches 80°C (176°F), remove from the heat and leave to cool.

The pastry
Meanwhile, using a round cookie cutter, cut out discs from the sheet of puff pastry large enough to line 8–10 holes of a shallow cupcake tin. Pour the cooled custard into the pastry cases (shells) and bake in a preheated oven, 220°C (425°F), Gas Mark 7, for 20 minutes. Serve the *pastéis de nata* warm, dusted with cinnamon and/or with icing (confectioners') sugar.

3 eggs

dust with sugar

English muffins

ENGLAND

The unmistakable delicate aroma of bergamot oil wafts by as teaspoons clink in cups of Earl Grey tea. A gentle good morning comes from English muffins with poached eggs.

300ml (10fl oz) milk
7g (¼oz) fast-action dried yeast (instant yeast)
25g (1oz) brown sugar
50g (1¾oz) butter or margarine, softened
425g (15oz) plain (all-purpose) flour
1 teaspoon salt
fine yellow polenta (cornmeal) or semolina flour, for sprinkling
oil, for greasing
eggs, to poach

Makes 8–10 muffins
Preparation time: 30 minutes, plus 1½ hours rising
Cooking time: 20 minutes

The muffins

Gently warm the milk in a saucepan. Remove from the heat, add the yeast and sugar and stir well. Leave for 5 minutes. Mix the softened butter or margarine with the yeast mixture, flour and salt in a bowl until you have a smooth, firm dough. Cover with clingfilm (plastic wrap) and leave to rise in a warm place for at least an hour until doubled in volume. Roll the dough out to a thickness of 2cm (¾ inch). Using a 5–8cm (2–3¼ inch) round cookie cutter, cut out discs of dough and place on a cookie sheet lined with nonstick baking paper. Sprinkle with a little polenta (cornmeal) or semolina flour, cover with a tea towel (dishcloth) and leave for a further 30 minutes or so. When they are ready, heat a frying pan thoroughly, oil it lightly and cook the muffins over a medium heat for 7–8 minutes on each side. Once cooked, cut them in half and toast them in a toaster or frying pan.

The poached egg

Bring 1 litre (34fl oz) of water to the boil in a saucepan with 1 tablespoon of vinegar and a pinch of salt. Stir with a spoon to create a whirlpool. Break the egg into a small bowl, then pour it gently into the centre of the whirlpool. Reduce the heat and keep the whirlpool going by stirring with a spoon. Cook for 2 minutes. Drain the egg with a slotted spoon and serve it on your English muffin.

Mangú

DOMINICAN REPUBLIC

If your senses are ready for a new adventure, you need only indulge them.
Try something new and exciting to start your day.

4 green plantains
950ml (32fl oz) boiling water
1½ teaspoons salt
25g (1oz) butter
1 large red onion
2 tablespoons olive oil

Serves 4
Preparation time: 10 minutes
Cooking time: about 30
  minutes

Peel the plantains and cut each into 8 pieces, first into quarters lengthways, then each quarter in half. Cook in the measured boiling water with the salt added until soft (how long this takes depends on how green the plantain is). Remove from the heat, drain and mash with a fork into a purée. Add a little cold water and the butter, and continue to mash until you have a smooth, thick and creamy consistency. Slice the onion and lightly fry in the oil in a pan. Now you can plate up your dish: arrange the purée as you wish and garnish with the fried onion.

Serve hot with fried eggs, fried cheese and toast.

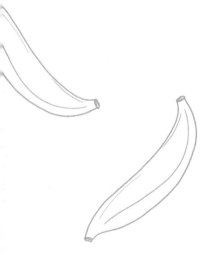

1 large onion

Blinis

RUSSIA

Simple, natural ingredients for a breakfast with old friends. It's late spring in rainy weather, with fur hats at the ready.

150g (5½oz) 00 flour
1 teaspoon fast-action dried
    yeast (instant yeast)
250ml (9fl oz) warm milk
1 egg
pinch of salt

Serves 6
Preparation time: 10 minutes,
    plus 1 hour resting
Cooking time: 15 minutes

Mix all the ingredients together in a large bowl. Cover with clingfilm (plastic wrap) and leave to rest for an hour.

Heat a nonstick frying pan, then spoon a small amount of the batter into the pan so that it forms a small round disc. When it starts to bubble on the surface, the underside is cooked. You can then turn your blini over and cook the other side. Repeat with the remaining batter.

In Russia, blinis are served with strawberry jam or with sugar and soured (sour) cream.

00 flour

warm milk

Cranachan

SCOTLAND

The tart note of the raspberries awakens the senses, like the north wind on a coastal walk. But then you are cosseted by clouds of cream, sweet honey and a soft tartan blanket.

100g (3½oz) porridge
    (rolled) oats
1 tablespoon white sugar
200ml (7fl oz) whipping or
    double (heavy) cream
150g (5½oz) Greek yogurt
1-2 tablespoons whisky
    (depending on taste)
about 200g (7oz) raspberries
4 teaspoons honey

Serves 4
Preparation time: 20 minutes
Cooking time: 1–2 minutes

Toast the oats in a frying pan – ideally nonstick – with the sugar for 1–2 minutes. Whip the cream, then fold in the Greek yogurt and the whisky.

Now you can assemble the cranachan in little glasses, starting with a layer of toasted oats, followed by the cream mixture and some raspberries. Repeat the 3 layers, and finish by topping each with a raspberry and a teaspoon of honey.

If you would prefer a more alcoholic version, you can add an extra teaspoon of whisky directly to the oats and let them absorb it. If you fancy a more fruity dish, purée the raspberries and use whole berries only to decorate. Have fun and prepare it how you like it best!

decorate with a raspberry and a teaspoon of honey

camhanaich

early morning dawn

Tostada

SPAIN

~~~~~~~~~~~~~~~~~~~~~~~~~~~~~~~~~~~~~~

A dish that epitomizes authenticity, this is made using humble yet vibrantly coloured ingredients. It's a breakfast that admirably represents the spirited people of Spain. Olé!

~~~~~~~~~~~~~~~~~~~~~~~~~~~~~~~~~~~~~~

2 fresh tomatoes
1 garlic clove
2 tablespoons extra virgin olive oil
dried oregano
2–4 slices of white bread
4 slices of Serrano ham, chopped
salt

Serves 2–4
Preparation time: 10 minutes
Cooking time: 5 minutes

First, prepare the sauce. Wash the tomatoes and peel the garlic clove. Grate the tomatoes and garlic to make a coarse purée. Add 1 tablespoon of the oil and oregano and salt to taste.

Toast the bread slices, then drizzle them with the remaining oil. Spread the tomato sauce over them, and finally top with the Spanish dry-cured ham.

extra virgin olive oil

1 garlic clove

Crazy cake

UNITED STATES

This is like a magic potion. The recipe has few ingredients, which, taken individually, don't say much. But once combined they produce a full, rounded flavour - an aromatic chocolate moment just for you. If this isn't magic, then what is?

180g (6¼oz) self-raising (self-rising) flour
150g (5½oz) white sugar
1 teaspoon bicarbonate of soda (baking soda)
3 tablespoons (unsweetened) cocoa powder
pinch of salt
250ml (9fl oz) water
4 tablespoons sunflower oil
1 tablespoon white wine vinegar
icing (confectioners') sugar

Serves 4–6
Preparation time: 10 minutes
Cooking time: 30 minutes

Sift the flour into a bowl and add the sugar and bicarbonate of soda (baking soda). Mix until evenly combined. Then add the cocoa powder and salt and mix again.

Finally, add the liquid ingredients, being careful to mix them in well with a wooden spoon. Pour the batter into a greased 20cm (8 inch) round cake tin and bake in a preheated oven, 180°C (350°F), Gas Mark 4, for 30 minutes.

Remove from the oven and leave to cool before decorating as you like. A dusting of icing (confectioners') sugar is usually enough for this soft cake.

flour

sunflower oil

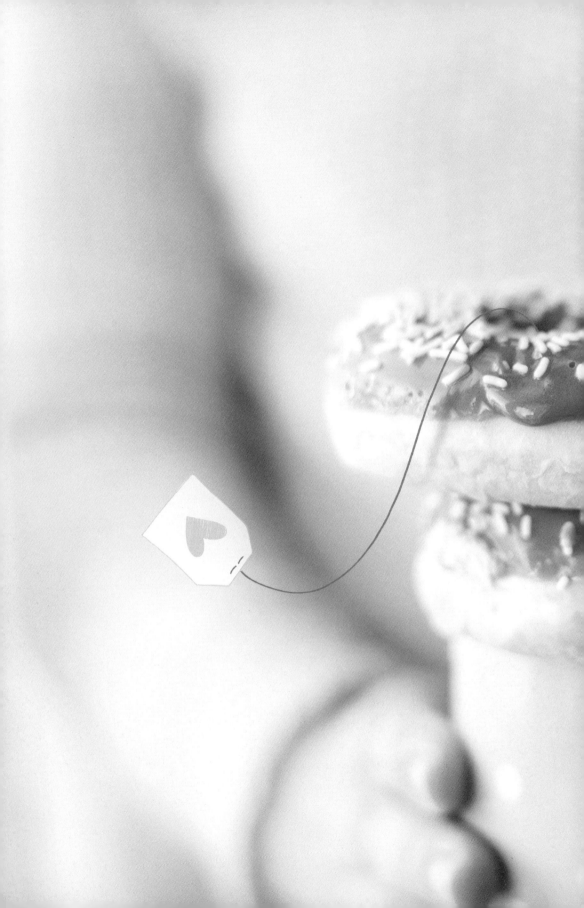

Doughnuts

UNITED STATES

~~~

Soft golden rings with an inviting sugary aroma and decorated in contrasting colours.
These are the ideal way to start the day in a happy mood.

~~~

500g (1lb 2oz) strong white flour
60g (2¼oz) white sugar
4 eggs
1 egg yolk
20g (¾oz) fast-action dried
   yeast (instant yeast)
seeds from 1 vanilla pod (bean)
70ml (4½ tablespoons) milk
80g (3oz) butter, softened
8g (⅓oz) salt
2 litres (68fl oz) vegetable oil

For the chocolate icing:
200g (7oz) plain dark
   (bittersweet) chocolate
20g (¾oz) butter

For the pink icing:
20g (¾oz) butter
180g (6¼oz) icing
   (confectioners') sugar, sifted
40ml (1½fl oz) water
2 drops pink gel food coloring

Makes 20–25 doughnuts
Preparation time: 15 minutes,
   plus 2¾ hours rising
Cooking time: 20 minutes

The dough

Mix the flour with the white sugar, eggs, yolk, yeast and vanilla seeds in a large bowl. Beat in the milk, a little at a time, until well combined. Add the butter and mix again to produce a smooth, firm dough. Knead in the salt, then cover with a clean tea towel (dishcloth) and leave to stand in a warm place for 45 minutes. Shape into balls of about 60g (2¼oz) each, cover and leave to rise in a warm place for about 2 hours until doubled in volume.

Using a 3cm (1¼ inch) round cookie cutter, cut a hole in the middle of each doughnut. Deep-fry the doughnuts, in batches, in the vegetable oil heated to 180°C (350°F) for 2 minutes on each side, then drain on kitchen paper (paper towels) and cool.

The icing

Meanwhile, for the chocolate icing (frosting), melt the chocolate and butter together in the microwave or in a heatproof bowl set over a saucepan of barely simmering water. Melt the butter for the pink icing, then mix it into the icing (confectioners') sugar. Gradually beat in the measured water and food colouring. When the doughnuts are lukewarm, ice the tops and decorate with sprinkles of your choice.

Kanelbullar

SWEDEN

The last leaves are falling on the windowsill as autumn (fall) gives way to winter. Wood crackles in the fireplace, and a sweet smell of cinnamon wafts in from the kitchen.

25g (1oz) fast-action dried yeast (instant yeast)
150ml (5fl oz) warm milk
85g (3oz) butter, softened
280g (9¾oz) plain (all-purpose) flour
70g (2½oz) white sugar
pinch of salt
pinch of ground cinnamon
1 egg, beaten
sugar crystals, for sprinkling

Makes 15 pastries
Preparation time: 40 minutes, plus 50 minutes rising
Cooking time: 5–10 minutes

Put the yeast in a bowl and stir in a little of the warm milk until dissolved. Mix in the rest of the milk and 60g (2¼oz) of the butter, then add the flour, a little at a time, kneading the dough with your hands. Finally, add 50g (1¾oz) of the sugar and the salt. Knead the dough vigorously for about 5 minutes until it stops sticking to the inside of the bowl.

Cover with clingfilm (plastic wrap) and leave to rise for 30 minutes, or until doubled in volume. Meanwhile, prepare the filling. Beat the remaining butter, sugar and cinnamon together until well combined and creamy.

Dust your work surface with flour and knead the dough some more, then roll it out into a rectangle. Spread the filling over it with a spatula. Starting from one longer side, gently roll up the dough into a log, then slice it into 15 thin slices and place on a baking tray (cookie sheet) lined with nonstick baking paper. Leave to rise, covered with a clean tea towel (dishcloth), for 20 minutes. Brush with the egg and sprinkle with sugar crystals. Bake in a preheated oven, 200°C (400°F), Gas Mark 6, for 5–10 minutes until golden.

cinnamon

Khao neow sangkaya

THAILAND

The sun's rays peep through the interwoven leaves of the palm grove. The wind catches the occasional crystalline drop in a pristine paradise. This dish bids you an enthusiastic "good morning" with a coconut aroma.

180g (6¼oz) black glutinous rice
1.25 litres (68fl oz) water
625ml (21fl oz) coconut milk
140g (5oz) brown cane sugar
　or palm sugar
4 eggs
salt
dessicated coconut or coconut
　milk, to decorate (optional)

Serves 6
Preparation time: 1 hour,
　plus overnight soaking
Cooking time: 50 minutes–
　1 hour

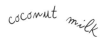

The rice

Wash the rice in cold water until it runs clear. Put it in a large bowl of cold water and leave to soak overnight. Drain the rice, put it in a saucepan with the measured water and bring to the boil. Then cover and cook over a low heat for 20 minutes. Drain the rice. Pour 250ml (9fl oz) of the coconut milk into a saucepan with 60g (2¼oz) of the sugar and a pinch of salt. Mix well and warm over a medium heat until the sugar has dissolved. Add the rice and cook over a low heat for a further 10–20 minutes. Turn the heat off and set aside to rest.

The custard

Mix the remaining coconut milk and sugar together with a pinch of salt in a saucepan and heat until the sugar has dissolved. Lightly beat the eggs in a bowl, pour into the coconut milk mixture and mix well. Pour the mixture into a 6-hole cupcake tin and place in a steamer. Steam for about 10 minutes. Remove from the heat and leave to cool. To serve, first place a layer of rice on the plate, then the cooked custard on top. Decorate with desiccated coconut or a spoonful of coconut milk, as you wish.

Menemen

TURKEY

The muezzin's call to prayer accompanies the sunrise, whose rays permeate this dish, giving it an extraordinary charge of energy.

4 tomatoes

oil

1 large onion, chopped

2 green (bell) peppers, cored, deseeded and finely chopped

4 eggs

1 teaspoon sweet paprika

chili powder (optional)

salt and pepper

Serves 2
Preparation time: 10 minutes
Cooking time: 15 minutes

Wash the tomatoes, make a cross-shaped cut in their tops and parboil in water for 1–2 minutes. Drain, peel and dice them. Pour a little oil into a large frying pan, add the onion and sauté for a couple of minutes. Add the tomatoes and peppers and cook for 10 minutes. Meanwhile, beat the eggs with a pinch of pepper and the paprika, season with salt and chili powder, if using, and pour the mixture into the pan.

Stir from time to time until the eggs are cooked. Serve with fresh crusty bread. Very tasty!

sweet paprika

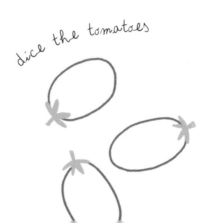

dice the tomatoes

Krumplis pogácsa

HUNGARY

The first few hours of the weekend pass slowly, and a warm, welcoming ambiance helps you relax.

600g (1lb 5oz) potatoes
15g (½oz) lard
450g (1lb) 00 flour
1 egg, beaten
salt

Serves 6–8
Preparation time: 20 minutes
Cooking time: 40 minutes

Wash the potatoes and dice them. Cook in salted boiling water for about 20 minutes until soft. Drain and leave to cool. Once cold, crush the potatoes and add the lard. Mixing carefully, add the flour a little at a time, working the mixture until it forms a soft, dense dough.

Roll the dough out on a work surface dusted with flour and brush all over with the beaten egg. Using a small round cookie cutter, cut the dough into discs. Place on a greased baking tray (cookie sheet) and bake in a preheated oven, 220°C (425°F), Gas Mark 7, for 20 minutes.

Serve the *pogácsa* warm with a cup of milky coffee.

potatoes

lard

Kunun gyada

NIGERIA

~~~~~~

*This dish would be the result if you managed to capture the sun in a box –
an explosion of colour and energy!*

~~~~~~

50g (1¾oz) short-grain rice
150g (5½oz) peanuts
tamarind juice, to taste
600ml (20fl oz) water

Serves 6
Preparation time: 10 minutes,
   plus at least 8 hours soaking
Cooking time: 10 minutes

Soak the rice in cold water for at least 8 hours, and the peanuts, separately, for 3 hours and drain.

If you are using fresh tamarind, soak it in hot water until it has softened, then crush in a fine-mesh wire sieve to extract the juice. Alternatively, use a few drops of ready-squeezed juice.

Blend the peanuts in a blender or food processor with 400ml (14fl oz) of the measured water, then extract the liquid by straining through a sieve lined with muslin (cheesecloth). (You can use the solid residue in other recipes, such as cookies or cakes.) Then blend the rice with the remaining water and set aside. Now pour the peanut milk into a small saucepan and start to warm it over a medium heat, stirring constantly so that it doesn't stick. When it boils, add the blended rice and cook for 20–25 minutes, continue stirring. Finally, add the tamarind juice. Cook for a further minute. Your peanut milk is ready to serve.

For a thicker and quicker version, blend the peanuts with a little water and soak the rice in hot water for 30 minutes, then cook everything together over a low heat for 35–40 minutes until the rice disintegrates. The result will be more like porridge (oatmeal). Both are delicious. Serve with fresh fruit.

peanuts and rice

Acknowledgements

Thousands of times I have imagined writing these words. Now that the time has come to do so, of course they are elusive, like shy little girls.

The first huge, heartfelt "thank you" is for you, Elisa. Because without your truly creative mind, your great passion and your talent, none of this would ever have seen the light. We've been through so much during this journey on paper: we have weathered creative storms, and navigated across seas of unknown ideas. We have been a compass for each other, a critical but honest mirror, a shoulder to lean on in moments when we felt lost or uncomfortable, and a release of adrenaline at moments of rejoicing. In case you were wondering, my bag is already packed, ready for the next journey.

The second – but no less important – "thank you" goes to our superb travelling chefs, Lorenza and Ludovica. Without your hands, your suggestions, your unfailing availability and generosity, this journey would not have been possible. Thank you for having travelled with us and allowing yourselves to be transported into our world.

We would like to thank our publisher, Nomos Edizioni, for having believed in our project and giving us the chance to put together a world of flavours, images and colours. And for having grasped, even before we did, a vision for eyes hungry for magic, creativity and good food.

Thank you to my closest friends – in no particular order, Chiara, Serena and Marzia – for having opened the doors to your homes, for having literally cradled all these ideas in your hands and for your indispensable moral support.

Heartfelt thanks to my family – especially you, Marcello. I could not wish for a more wonderful brother. Finally, with all my heart, thank you to you, Marco. For the love with which you nourish me every day, for the time you have devoted to this project, the faith you are always ready to have in me and for all the great laughs!

Laura

It's strange how an idea comes into being and then changes along the way – how its development can surprise you if only you give it the chance. This book represents much more than the realization of a project on paper; it has been a veritable journey, bringing with it profound changes. When realizing a complex project such as this one, it isn't just a matter of going beyond your own stylistic and technical limits, but also of bringing your feelings into play, giving them free rein and above all sharing them with a new language.

Here, too, it is a case of rediscovering the beginner's mentality (shoshin), one free of the habits of the "expert", one that is open.

I would like to extend my heartfelt thanks to those who have made this journey possible.

Thank you to Laura, for the unique atmosphere of her pictures, but even more for her sharing of meals, doubts and dreams. You know what it has meant to me to have you by my side over these years.

Thank you to Lorenza and Ludovica, for setting sail with us and for knowing how to infuse each dish with the right dose of magic.

Thank you to Emanuele and Benedetta (Nomos Edizioni) for believing in us from the start, leaving us to explore new worlds and showing us the way.

Thank you to Nicolò, my ally in this life. You know.

Thank you to my invaluable four-legged assistants and life teachers. It is astonishing what an animal can bring to the life of each of us. However busy our lives may be, their gaze is always ready to meet ours and bring us back to something that is true.

Ishin-denshin,
(from one heart to another).